T0126361

Room Where I Get What I Want

Room Where I Get What I Want

by S. Whitney Holmes

Black Ocean
Boston · New York · Chicago

Black Ocean
P.O. Box 52030
Boston, MA 02205
blackocean.org

Cover Art by Josh Wallis | joshwallis.com
Book Design by Nikkita Cohoon | nikkita.co

ISBN 978-1-939568-10-6

Library of Congress Cataloging-in-Publication Data

Holmes, S. Whitney
[Short stories. Selections]
Room where I get what I want / S. Whitney Holmes.
    pages cm
ISBN 978-1-939568-10-6 (alk. paper)
I. Title.
PS3608.O4943556A6 2015
813'.6~dc23
                                   2015007129

FIRST EDITION

CONTENTS

II. Method of Loci

It was like the classic dream where you dream there's one more room to your house—silly me, it's been there all the while, and what? I'd forgotten? A whole other room!

–Joy Williams

The House That Is Not a House

is right here on top of the cheerleading pyramid.
The house is consuming fewer vegetables
and more Russian novels every day. The house is
on the shelf beside a matching book collection
with blue leather and gold embossed lettering.
It's been hollowed out to hide a gun.
The house that is not a house lords over
the mangled birds' bodies, keeps a knotty blue
birdie foot under its tongue. The house is everlasting.
It knows something about God it doesn't wish to share.
The house that is not a house didn't kill the birds,
but it wanted to. The house that is not a house
believes in reincarnation and dreams
of becoming a stapler. The house is wearing
a fancy new pillbox hat today
with a matching clutch to hold its No. 2 pencils.
The house that is not a house embraces
its negative distinctions. The house is not
a house of fire. The house is not a house
of the budding sexuality of those to be slain in horror films.
The house is not a house of love leaves, a house
of mother's antique glassware, a house of muzzleloaders.
It is not a house of hickory-smoked anything, a house built
of paperwork, a house formed from the tinny rings
and rotary gurgles of the world's discarded phones.
The house that is not a house is nothing but a house.
At night, its tiny wail decorates the trees.
If you sleep with one arm in Istanbul
and a toe in a swimming pool in Hollywood, you'll see.

I.

One Dressform to Another

You'll never guess the names of these insects
in my chest. I'd tell you *heart*, but it wouldn't be
                    true. Some things take years.

            In the dim light of a lamp I thought antique,
                    I see the shade's machined stitches. See
my mother's wrought hand was made to hold you.
            O lips, you curl like a baby! You shake like a girl!

Meet mother. She will like you more than me.
            It is hard-wired in her to hate the nails
dragged down the canal, the lump that would make friends.

            Friend, I am always telling.
Chew my fingers. Squint and roll. Tongue the raisins.
Don't curse, and she'll love you.
            Stop with the cup at your lip.

Obviator

Because I have watched you alphabetize your book collection
I believe it's all true—the bulb, the split, the weeds
gathering at the corner of your mouth

                       (little white

     *

lies).   Ours is the movie where the action
        hero, sensing the thug's gnarly fist,
takes me in his mouth to sweeten the blow.

     *

You sit in the grass, swigging red wine from the bottle and eating
a tulip bulb like an onion. Your eyes don't even water.
I watch you from knee deep in the hydrangeas.

     *

Sometimes you in the next room is even better than you here.

     *

I could watch you alphabetize your book collection
for months—it's only half sarcasm.

(Would you bifurcate the statement
or scoop empty the middle like a kiwifruit?)

                    *

You don't even know how much that swollen bulb cost someone.

Heroes know nothing of cost, just the caught
chances, safe dangers, a line of condoms
like a Jacob's ladder, a ladder

                    *

unbuilding itself, ladder of lost rungs.

We are bound by nothing consequential—ah, yes!
You seize outcome with superhuman limbs!

                    *

More like a flystrip than a ladder.

                    *

Early Persians held that red tulips were a declaration.
Yellow for the hopeless, and tulips
with a black center for a heart
burnt by love. I am glad

*

you ate the not-yet—I am!

Good what's grown hasn't a physical root from which to flower.

My love, my hero—!

*

You have trouble telling when I am sincere

but you are not alone.

In the Garden When You Look from the Corner of My Eye

The unicorns don't care we're not virgins
            so we break their horns off. We're surprised
to find them hollow, and once we discover they make lousy kazoos,
            we fill the bony cones like glimmering cornucopias,
low-sweeping primrose and butternut squash
            spilling out their ragged mouths.

                    You are drunk with tipping the buttercups.
            I desire to fuck everything
                            I see, but I'm scared of the thorns.
            I let you braid a lock of unicorn mane in my hair instead.

        Some things will never grow back. This is why
some women draw their eyebrows on. This is why

when we whip our heads around so fast our hair hits us
            in our faces, we manage to see where we are.

At the Ramp Festival

Your maw will be smarting.
An orange reminds you.

Nothing in your mouth
but a tongue. In your chest, the swallow.

Father says *Take this and eat*, fear of your mother
growing. When your lips move

to flap a song, you're there
again. Basket brimming wild

leeks for frying with the potatoes.
Mason jar of bacon grease. No matter

how many times you wash, your hands
remain greased. And if you eat ramps

raw on Friday, there's no school on Monday.
The stench takes days to leave your sweat.

At the ramp feed, hairy bulbs fetch pennies.
Medusas plot in the belly,

miles between your nose
and the onion's garlic rot.

The smell will inch down your follicles.
You'll want an orange bath,

an excuse for missing church. You'll leave
the skunk weeds in the yard, upturned,

scared sick of the earth, scared sick of the grimy hand.

Room That Is My Mother

When I heard a vowel the first time
I placed my ear to the inside O
      of the body and looked out.

I hadn't known we were full of rooms.

When I emerged there was a whole world
      where I used to be, rot wood
            where I used to be, and nothing

in my own space but curling
         ribbon drawn over a scissor,
pulled to spring.

I don't need anything I haven't given myself. My resolve:
      a thin shawl just for looks.

      What will my hands be but opening doors?

Rubin's Vase

At first, we were simply trying to forget our bodies.

        The boys jeered: *Hey, get a load of Vase-Face!*
            But how many could pinch

daffodil stems between the tips of their noses?
        Jealous of our cover-girl pouts and well-formed chins,
                         the creep
            of ambiguity in relationship, depth,
our seamless contours
        with the power to make a vessel of space

between us. This is how we got here:

        we noticed.
The muscles of a torso rearranged themselves.
        We stared into the cradle, felt special
before we saw it was one-size-fits-all, a nook

like the weak spot on the women's room
            door that won't lock, gives way
        under a foot wedged there for privacy—
we could each be any woman with pants around her knees.

        We pulled each other's hair

to know we'd never be less separate, to know our definitions
like favorite books whose spines never break.

We became hard-backed. Lost our backs entirely.
Because what did we need them for.

Method of Loci: Grocery List with You and the House on Kentucky Avenue

In the doorway of my mother's house, you
crucify a corn cob, pulling back the husk
to nail to the doorframe. The cob hangs
erect to greet me. *Hello, again. Hello.*

On opening the TV cabinet, I find
your thick wrist sticks out, your hands
baked whole into panettones. You puppet
the loaves to dance a saltarello
over the couch, their raisin eyes squinting.

And in my childhood bedroom you force
feed eggs to my stuffed animals.
Teddy's sour face twisted,
yolk in his furry snout.

Then in the shower peeling
an orange. Its rough skin fallen to the tile
wraps the little hairs on your toes.
When you get inside, past the bitter
white scruff to where the fruit should be,
there isn't a shriveled wedge to suck.
Instead it's Pop Rocks, hissing
shrapnel wrapped in rind, and mini-
marshmallows to air-bag the blow.

What were you ever doing
in my mother's house? Asking,

Why remember the grocery list like this
when you could write it down?

To have forever.
To have what you have done.

House Tells History

Before fingernails' thin nacre,
I was a need. Before I was a thought,
         someone bore cold and rain.

Did the garden decorate me? Or
                        did I spare a patch of the forest I paved?

Because fencing begat ballet, I wished
         to make art of a fight. A pirouette
could have carried me up a spiral stair—

         But because I was begotten of need, ornament came later.
                  As a kind of foreplay. A whisper
slipped in the ear. Broken glass in a pianist's pocket.

                  I trialed and errored. I grew
                  to fit mountains in my mouth. Now,

         I am a mean bird and nothing—neither the smooth tips of practice
arrows nor their neon plastic feathers—can find me in the dense-leafed sky.

                  Anymore, I don't know where I am.

         Like momentous wooden gates, my eyes,
                        who knows if they're open at all?

A Tongue in a Mouth of Teeth Is a Powerful Muscle

More people are killed by falling coconuts than by sharks.

Creationists tell us animals were not carnivorous before The Fall.

The dinosaurs' long teeth were necessary for opening coconuts.

Teeth like sharks' sawing the sea's strange bodies.

The would-be teeth in a chicken embryo's beak.

Our science begins by unbuilding the bird.

We find in the chicken teeth and tails like the old T-Rex's.

We find sharks were all once apples in God's great eye.

Along the beach, the children collect sharks' teeth in Dresden teacups.

Scientists tell us sharks don't like the ways we taste,

while my people are killed by falling coconuts.

My hands are falling coconuts and this

tea tastes, gently, of bitter anise.

My people are dying for a weapon.

Or a tongue, or a tail

too strong to tuck between their legs. The coconuts tell us nothing.

My palms turn red in fall. My people—

found starving with the shore by the sharks—

I have them eating out of my hands.

As a Child Obeying

Victorian sofas covered in plastic,
       a piano with its shoulder
              tipped up, teeth grinning, a frail yellow
              lamp with a pull chain.

       I ache to perform.
Mother is saying, *don't touch, don't touch,*
in time with the pulsing blender.

Spring Elegy

1.

I walk with it in my step. That was the spring that was every spring. The snow
couldn't keep its white head out of our business. Our bodies tired
warming to the medicine dusted everywhere, and everywhere
numbing. Film at the backs of our throats. Film rolling our mistakes
back on a loop.

On an interminable loop,
that was spring. Birds committed suicide to get back at me, flung
beak-first to the pavement at my feet. *See what you've driven us to. See.*
And the absence of song sounded like a song, a one-two *whee-ooo*
kamikaze cry as they squeezed their fat breasts

between the grills of passing cars. The measured inhales
finding their body parts strewn—
forked foot hanging by one hooked claw from the low-slung electrical wire,
wing and a quarter of a torso broken on the mailbox.
I got used to it after a while. *There's another one.*

2.

That was just spring. I learned the airport is paved with dead deer
and the best course of action is to keep an accurate count.
The best course is
turn around and never get on the plane. Forget
I said that. That was the spring we picked my grandfather up

slack by his elbows, slipped him
into a cardigan, bones poking against skin like splinters wrapped in cloth.
His body an oversized wing. *That thin, yes—that.*

3.

I have always been ungrateful. I was never,
never any different. Eat after me. The bird feathers'
furious thud on the windshield. *These are our bodies, broken for you.*
Take a seat. The best animals made me
flinch, their bodies' flit, fitting together to prove they were alive
and always the threat of stillness, always annoying songs begging I follow
such sad instruction. Grief is for the birds. *This is how,* I tell them.
This selfish. This broken.

A Gallery

I never intended to be all dressed up.
I never intended to run into you at the party.

I tried to match the floor's polished stone.
I came across as something of a gag. Chignon at the nape,
              my spine's channel run slick into a dress. To impress
                       you was never my intention.
To enhance the setting,

snow covered mud. You wouldn't know if I didn't tell you.
There were no windows in the whole loft. Or maybe
      you did. No—the weather had little to do
      with our hair. We wanted a stir. We tied our collections on
      tightly, laces

                  done up. Fastened our jaws. Perhaps
you knew the snow outside, the likelihood.
My presence. If I didn't wonder at
your shoes' sudden shine, my faces looking up.

Room without Walls

To become weightless you must come down
faster than you went up. Whereas gravity is
broken, you are broken. At once, they'll find out
everything. Your bedsheets will submit to
blacklight. Your closet will picnic in the park shelter.
The dogs in their backyard houses
will turn their noses up at the moon.

Forget loyalty. You can't float with a foot
on the ground. Lower your shoulders
faster than they crept inside your ears.

*

Remember you wanted this to begin with

a word taking possession of your body:

annex (n): the seizure sewing you to a pillow.
Your fall like candy from a shaken box.
Effortless as a ring slipped from a small finger.

Definition 3, *an appendix*. P.S. of the document.
P.P.S. of the body. I've added this part for you.

*

When it works, it works, but—

Without weight, you needn't affix yourself
to anything, *to join in a subordinate capacity.*

As if *to honor and obey.*

Annex the sky for all I care. Measure it
with your long tape. Draw up
the paperwork.

*

I'll be up there, too
                alone. The air is big enough, and my lungs vast.

From this height, laughs cast
needle shadows.

*

Good riddance, feet on the ground!

Consider this dream
definition 4, *a supplementary building designed to supply extra*
accommodation for some special purpose; a wing.

Now. Spread your wings.
Find some special purpose.

                              *

The dream wing, which holds what it wants,
                    or the wing to hold the dream—

*

Finally, you can open your arms.
When there are no walls,
what you feel is not a *draught* but a *breeze.*

Pantry, Cans, and Jars

Kneading my knuckles in a not-yet bread,
I think of ways to repurpose my womb:

a purse that holds the moon,
wet and heavy dangling from a red
wrist; add a spout to make a wineskin
left in arid terrain, full sloshing
whoosh whoosh, the sound comforting
tiny-sandaled baby wise men;

and there must be a way to use a damp sack
that doesn't require holding: ripped and sewn
its cloth makes a pair of panties or a child's dress—
not so much holding as holding back;

dipped in bronze and mounted, my own
something important; skill; word; thing I'll never guess.

Love and Forgetting

One perceives the curve of a bowl as the raw egg sliding down its side.
The other perceives the egg as a galaxy, the uncanny sun some love
   to feel on their faces.

One calls across a distance, *Yoo-hoo! Hello, there!*
One calls from across the yard, *You, who?*

One prefers ornament and the closed-mouth kiss of morning.
One prefers the French horn not for its slick kiss, but the hand in
   its throat.

One stands waiting, expecting something. Food or a storm.
The other comes like a bear aroused by rushing feet.

On one's stomach in sleep, one faces the black cake one will become.
One steeps lavender in milk and beds down on the sea's stage whispers.

Peeling a banana, one is always posed in a thin white dress against a breeze.
One watches the other scoop the last bit of gelatin from a Depression-
   glass dish.

One never considers the possibility of one's self
as a wasp or a wicker loveseat. One rarely asks.

Love is so short,
and forgetting is so long.

One sees a woman on her side, her stomach like pudding in the dark.
One sees nothing but the moon-drawn tide of one's own body
   trespassing into the night.

Obviator

This time, I brought opera glasses.
I see more clearly. Beside you,

      *

a picnic basket. A bottle.
Some grass. You sat
swigging red wine from the bottle
and ate a tulip
bulb like an onion.

      *

I watched, hidden in the flowers.
Did I dream the bottle up?
Did you sit in the grass
with two glasses, but I never
came, so you drank
straight from the bottle?

      *

I am full of reason
to doubt my reasoning.

So I look to you,

*

and a bed of flowers glisten
because you arrived early
to spray them with water,
a handful of glitter mixed in—you know how much
I love a thing that glows.

So you were

*

waiting, and I was hiding.

When another hour had passed
and my legs ached from crouching,
your hands were tight, and the wine was
gone. You tossed a piece of chocolate cake

in my direction. (Did you see me there?
Did you think you could

*

bait me?)

And when that hour had passed, and I hadn't
made a move for the cake, though it was lovely
crosshatched with green blades of grass—

*

With another hour passed, you thrust
your tight hands into the tighter earth, clawed
deeper, shook loose a tulip bulb not yet flowered.

You shook it loose, shook loose
the dirt from around the bulb and bit
in half, hard, fast, swallowed whole
the half, the thing

    *

I could pretend not to see. Through these glasses,
the colors beside you:

      (You know how
      nostalgic I am

    *

         for things of which
         I never was a part)

yellow and red flowers, a gingham throw under
the live oak, and beyond the edge of the park,
a stack of books fastened with a belt.

World, Prepare Me

to be a sanctuary,
          a gob-let-gob world at my lips.

World spun sapphire by sugar-stained glass.

World of my lover
entered slowly gobbled gone and down.
                    World of sound.

                    Sound of a world sluiced—

And so the world of my lover in my mouth,

          scoffed down. World washed down
                    with Scotch swill washed down with bird.

Of a bird in my body, its wide
                    calcified wingspan, iliac crest,

          what is left? What leaves?

World of swish,
          sound of a world inside which nothing sticks.

The Worst of Moving Is Boxes of Books

We trip
over the faucet drip. We lift
with our backs. Cradle sweat.

A storm beats rubber wrists
on the windows. Bang
all night, we're gonna

buy new ones,
air-tight. Gonna burn
the box that holds the toaster

oven. Singe our hair
for English muffins.
The elephant I thought I had

has had itself.
The room in the middle
of the elephant

is warm and sweats
a fluid to break us down.
Between elephant belly walls

and a particle-board bookcase
hardly more than the sum
of its particles, a discourse

heats up, digests
the old wisdom. Yes,
that conversation grows tiresome.

Inasmuch as our house has a little
girl with rabbit stickers
on her fingernails, I have

a little girl. Don't tell me
home is the number
of neckties hung in the closet

when I know
it's the capacity for holding
neckties. I hold your foot

to my ear and expect an ocean,
a house built for more
people to sit in a family room.

I count two.

Disappears Again

I am all paid up on attention.

      Here: My argyles fold like paper. The books destroyed
                 in the basement flood are shelved in rows, spines
   shrunken half-circles, bulking
bodies packed tight. To play Memory,

      spread the cards
               face down. Then: *turn turn* match
      or: *turn turn* no match and reset.

     What's the point that won't stay still
          and doesn't want me? But always
it wants me. Entices me with cleansing grapefruit
scents and wind chimes. What's the point

                that once it swallows me, it spits?

I am tired and need a place to lie down.

Mistaken for Someone Else

Balloon string loops around my wrist, birthday cake face.
A chair is now a loof. A bird is now a twink. A man is now a boot.

Something sinister sighs in the cereal box.
Spine wrenches. Gut tingles.

No, I never...

When my feet turn red in the shower, suck
a wet chunk of hair. Curly straw. Eat this. Drink that.

Syringes poke from wine glasses in a soapy sink.
And one between my teeth!

Sure, I wanted to, but...

Whinny. Neck broke like a fish and swum up the drain.
Flop. My fingers flip like pipefish.

A butter pat on the tongue melts in a slow dirty sweep.

A door becomes a blink. Please, one blink.

Inside Your Head Is a Map of Your House
and Inside That Map Is Where You Actually Live

Where I live, love rolls off the tongue like a licorice candy spat in a penny pond. Children dance around the town fountain to the staccato notes of trombones. At the center of the fountain, lips pursed, you pose Poseidon-like atop a hippocampus. In your rucksack, a hundred drowned horses' heads lolling. What do you think? You hone your trident over their flat-rock teeth. What do you do? You think.

*

Where I live, you'd believe. All's a cluttered grayscale. I leave my rooms each morning to collect. In the air, burning tires. In the watering cans, gasoline. In you, prayer like a foot in my mouth. Wheeling round disks of bread in my wheelbarrow, I think about going on strike. I do not go on strike. I think about moving to Florida.

*

Where I live we get naked. I rub the bread all over your body. It's like pumice tearing down the bricks of your thighs, which are flushed and dotted with crumbs. Bits of broken skin. It's like thinking and then all at once it's like doing. Abrasive. Stale.

Fills with Water, Neck Deep

I've tried to tell before how I got here and failed. I know this is the room,
because your arms hang like fat worms on a hook, and you've left

your shoes and socks in my mouth. Remember? I'm not holy enough
        to continue.
        Especially with you. You say, *Empty*

the fish tank. Limp bodies of sea
        dragons like colored weeds and a big goldfish named Buddha
        dot the shiny floorboards (so shiny
                    I couldn't have cleaned them myself).

                (O the furniture! O all of it! I've never kept a house,
      but here the piles of dirty panties aren't tall enough to hide behind.)

I gather the fish bodies in the dry tank and pour pitchers
over them. Am I empty when their bellies jolt and they blink
thick blinks?
        As empty as holy. Of course, their googley eyes gaggle. They open
                their mushy lips. Buddha's mouth swallows
                the lovely couches that littered my youth.

Cave

What have you done to get here, here?
        The list is longer than a matchstick.

What have you done with joy, joy?
        A lullaby rocking boat
        tethered to my thigh.

What have you sewn to the inner curtain of your eye?
        A passage full of open doors.
        The canary going on and on.

What have you lost on the pebbled lake's bottom?
        What I have ever done with joy.

Parlor

I arrived   In hopes of remembering

This ugly thing   I have

With stickers   Stuck to what I know of pockets

And Blow Pops   The treasures they keep hidden

A newfound sweetness   Poured from her loosely

Lined lips   On her deathbed I was afraid

It wasn't true   That I hated her

Every moment   Dismissive

With a yo-yo   Flick of the wrist

I clung to   Stories bound in leather

The old woman   Wearing the wolf

Who understood   I could love

What I hated   Most

Was my mother   The world I hoped to touch

Apology for Apologies

Decided to
stop apologizing.

Found you
on the roof.
On the roof, dragged

and wet in your navy
coat. Wool up
to your chin.

Like the winter
air taking
refuge

from its own
coldness, I filled
your chest.

Bovine Disposal Debate Rages
West Milford, WV, May 2006

Week One

We laugh about a dead cow rotting in the river.
We follow the story, in love with its movements.

The folks in West Milford don't even think *aliens*
or *exsanguination*, the point not death, but disposal.

The carcass a modular home piece plopped
water logged in the West Fork River,
tough hide, stews for days.

No one hauls up a finger.

No farmer comes forward to claim his ward.

Dirt kids poke with pawpaw sticks, the trees'
rotten flowers jacket their toes. They slice
the brown fruit with pocket knives and chuck
the seeds. Mostly, it's the smell.

Responsibility begs belonging in our hair.

The DEP assures us our water
does not suffer for a cow.

Because it's snagged upstream
from the dam, it's not wild, not cash,
not bearer bonds or fencable jewelry.
No one knows what agency to call.

Week Two

Press your lips to water and trust it is not dirty.

Think about boiling our water,
just in case, but our arms are weak
and our pots cast iron.

This is our house, you say, won't let
what's out there get in us.

How is our bath water?
How is your nose in the bath water?
How is your nose tipped in the bath,
lips trilling bubbles, solvent for skin?

Week Three

Someone has to take the bull by the horns.

Finally, the firemen.

Yellow coats line up
vespers. Toss cedar wood,
hyssop sprig, bit of red yarn.
They build that which
it is their occupation to destroy.

We place the animal's ashes in our water
to sprinkle seven times with a sprig around the house,

over the little impatiens nodding in barrels.

Wash ourselves, our clothes, wait for evening
to make us clean of the death we've held.

We've done it by numbers, but finger

all night the house's quiet. The bruises
yellowing our thighs when pushed. Tooth
hung loose by a string around the doorknob.
Eyelash fallen on our pillow—

is it your wish or mine?

Our Agreement

The praying mantis on the porch
is not so unsettling as surprising. And a little drunk,
I am happy to stand on your porch
looking at this little green beast—
not thrust into our day, but folded from grass,
a sweet whistle if we put our lips to it,
arranged at the corner of our evening, turned
to pose for my camera. Its face lovely, mean,
like yours. Its face, my god! The old religion
of the colored capsules that bloom sponge dinosaurs
when left in a glass of water. I used to run them
under the hot tap to speed it up. Now—
I would go back. I would drop them
in a glass and watch their long necks eke out.
Would have you with me in an oversized T-shirt
to stand in watch. To know by the quiet measure of a sponge
grown big with whatever's around, you must
love me this way. Silent and looking at something else.

Aubade

Rising into last night's quiet blue
dress, I slung on my spine like slack rope.
The sun pulled on the horizon
like a sturdy boot to trudge up the sky, and I
played over how best to lounge without care come night
and the party, to nod and smile with a single cheek.

I try to catch the setting sun in a bedsheet
pinned to the line, but the linen's taut belly is full
of wind. I slip a pair of panties in your suitcase,
a lacy accident nestled against your sensible socks.
I can't stop your going but I can stop you
doing it with pleasure.

I'll pull on my old boots and follow
your car to the end of the avenue.
I will be filled with such wisdom as why
light is best left to the moon.
Nothing is ever as lovely
as when it's reflected off its absence.

Given a Hand

I have decided I am the agent.
I make the action.
Whose tongue in whose cheek?

I care. I do.

What I think of forever:

An opening, a fire. When you will cover
        a knoll centuries deep, the dead stir will make
you think of me, mound filling
        small of your back.
Take mouth to me.

And hands. I have decided I am
the agent. I do the doing.   Do this.

Forgive me. I bleed.
I was bloody when I arrived.

Room Where I Get What I Want

I come when you slip a finger in my mouth.
I come when you lose your balance, a finger in my mouth.

I come when you muscle a finger in my mouth.
I come when you twist somebody's arm all the way and make 'em say
      uncle please, a finger in my mouth.

I come when you elbow a finger in my mouth.
I come when you blackmail, with pictures of a finger thrown to the hard
      wet tongues of other women's mouths, this finger in my mouth.

I come when you won't take no for an answer.
I come when you fold back my lips like a groomer and scrutinize my
      canines with a finger in my mouth.

I come when you make me talk dirty around a finger in my mouth.
I come when you tell me say *Yeh yeh yeh* through my nose because
      a finger's in my mouth.

I come when you suck on a bar of soap, ask where'd I learn
that word a grimy finger in my mouth.

I come when you flash a shrunken head snug against your soft palate and
   tongue. It's *my* shrunken head, my very head but shrunken, mine
   as the finger in my mouth.

I come when you fold me up dig hands into my clavicles say *Mine* and
   squeeze me hard. Because then I own you. You're as mine as the
   finger in my mouth.

Quantum Leap

—into your histories of touching women.

The easter-egg midriff counting her freckles in the mirror.

—into the wide-mouthed navel who rode the bus in stilettos.

—into this one, her name was? I wear her like a wig.

The knees collecting layers of nail polish.

The crooked nose who drank moonshine and knew crosswords from memory.

—into the purple one. Did she coo or grunt?

I can be that. There. Lovely yellow dress. I can wear that.

Bobby pins playing muzak on your ribcage, big teeth and shiny.

—into the clavicles dancing to the faucet drip.

Your momentary airplane. I am the moment.

The zipper spine who spoke oceans on cable access, neat chignon, hairnet.

—into the button knuckles who wore earrings in the shower.

I can be her, fumbling on the doorstep with a baguette in the bag.

Ankles doing god knows what.

I can plunge my hand inside, spread my fingers like a grade school turkey.

My nose stuck in a bouquet of elbows.

Read you in Braille across rows of nipples.

Ankles doing what? Yes!

I have been known to worship.

Bony, slink, light, blue.

Bind my breasts. I can fill space.

If I call myself you, I become you—

Fever.   Tongue.   Finger.

And what have you to offer me?

Obviator

You sat in the grass swigging
red wine from the bottle
and you know the rest.

Before, when I said I was glad, I wasn't

      *

being sarcastic. Or rather,
I was, but I've stopped.

I have watched you for months.
I have watched you plant
the bulb inside yourself

      *

so I won't have to grow.

I have often tied myself,
each foot, each red hand,

to a horse. I have spooked and ridden
paradox, lover I meet when

*

you leave me pregnant with defeat.

My love, my hero, you have gone

*

ahead of me, cut a path through the thicket.
And I am just about to join you.
I am almost on my way.

II. Method of Loci

The built house unbuilds itself
each night, draws the drapes
like a hot bath. Undressed
in a claw-foot tub, its creaking
eases into morning.

And dressing, forgets
its rings by the sink.

This much dream is an extra room.
Everywhere I've lived, I've dreamed the room.
Its space is the space after

my terrycloth tennis shoes,
the diorama I built in their box:

horses in fixed gallop,

river running like open scissors.

The method of loci is sometimes called
a memory palace. Fill the familiar
blueprint with whatever you need
to remember. In this way,
Germany's Clemens Mayer
memorized 1,040 random digits
in a half hour.

He walked around his house.

I am building something.
            I thought

it was already built.   It was
chateau. It was schloss
        alcazar,   citadel.
It was castle,   fortress,
and garage apartment.
                    It was,
it will   be nest.

The built house unbuilding
draws the first place like drapes.
It hides its claws. It creaks
like an old house, but what's so
old about an old house?

Each forgetting dresses
the sink with rings.

It had been years since I lived
in that house when I dreamed
the walls were full of wild men.
　　　I was not
allowed inside. I only peeked, my feet
still touching my side of the line,
the worn brown carpet
in my mother's living room. Still one
wild man saw me

　　　　　　　　　—a streak of hair.

The sun like a pink eraser takes
back the night's etching. In the dark,
I can believe in you.

I am building a palace and here you are
in flannel pajamas, turning down the bed.

I didn't invite you
here to sleep.

When they fall in love, builders build
pedestals. I build a house
for you to live in.

Long-haired men draw a circle
on the inside of the wall;
                    there is an eye.

They draw another and there are two.
Draw a rectangle and there is a door.
Draw my profile and learn the secret
of sawing a woman in half.

I use rainbow blocks
to build the house. Pieces
spread across hard wood
floors will make their way
under a couch. I find rooms
I put there for the dust.
Find weekends spent constructing

inverted catenary arches
and hyperboloid structures,
the curve of a pilgrim's
bonnet for an awning.
Find Rococo mirrors and shells,
both little rooms to buttress off of.
Find memories belonging
to some lovers else.

Remember the diorama? I wanted to be
the plastic pilgrims standing dumb
while Indians gathered maize.
I wanted to be the horses' un-breath
in their horsey stares. To bisect
my house and pose
in an invitation to look.

I say who comes and goes.

My hands are birds in blue mittens.

I pressed my back against the door.
I felt a man through the drywall.
Felt all one feels of a wild man pressing,

the equal opposite of pressure
inside me. I kicked open

on the dotted line hinge,
wish to say I ran, but rather looked
rapt like a child through the wall
that I trusted once would hold me.

My attention to detail is lacking.

I am supposed to be in love.

I am supposed to have thought

many thoughts about architecture.

So it's about memory.
                              So think
something was left
in these rooms. Try to place
what's missing,

                    but to remember,
one must have known in the first place.

Sharpen your pencil on a wild man
and do the cartography.

Map the margins of motionlessness
with approximations of movement—

for example, sex is the most perfect way
to move without going anywhere.
In this way, I never traveled
through a dozen silver cities.

The shape—a pointy elbowed house
that bathes in mad fits of bubbles,
house that bends to bowl
all I want—my container takes!

Let's hurry to get
your mysteries off the shelf
before my book club comes over.

Clemens Mayer arrives to memorize
the litany of our embarrassments. He draws
a curtain on the wall like a flannel bath.
With relish, pulls it aside:

                              there,

the men lined up with capes of hair
around brick-built shoulders
hold hands, walkie-talkies tucked in their belts.
They bow in the applause of static sifted
through their radios, pull roses
from their underarms
to throw at our stocking feet.

Come night, we can look through the wall
and see which performance convinces.

How now to hold memory in dreams
of rooms dreamed up
to hold memories of dreams?

Come night, a cardboard room comes
scissor-river running.

A simple gable could carry the wall
up in a triangular termination
to receive the roof of a lover's sour mouth.

To run with diorama hands.

God, to run.

Come, diorama night. Come

bisect the first place, be swallowed by the wash
of shutters, smack-closed eyelids, the doorknob
bobs above bathwater tide like an island
my knee makes in ocean.

Come moon. When the sun comes down
here to rub us out, face me
like a pilgrim, your arms so full of corn
there is no room inside them.

So I'm full, too.
My dresser drawers are brimming
with unsharpened pencils.

Come night, come glue us
in the blue shoe box we loved in.

Come night   come glue us
come purse   come shoe box
Come strand of chili-pepper lights   come
crystal-covered pillow making grids of our cheeks
Come smoke alarm broadcasting kitchen mistakes
Come squirrels to attic   come wind chimes indoors
Come laundry come laundry come bones   Come
make me make myself at home   Make me leave
my shoes by the door   Come green-striped carpet
to pink-painted toes

Bananas browning atop the microwave   come
Faucet drip sink full of cutting boards   come
Fridge water pitchers and pickle jars   come
Pill bottles packed full of safety pins   come   Come
psychedelic bunny dress and fluorescent bulbs
Come magical orange cleaning each surface
Come house   come building   come design and fillings
Come bacon grease cup and toilet bowl cleaner
    Carpets for crumbs
to make significant nests in   come
come   Come locking the door
Come bearing a box   to fill with more

Acknowledgements

I'm grateful to the editors of the publications in which these poems first appeared: *32 Poems, Another Chicago Magazine, Barrelhouse, Cave Wall*, the *Cincinnati Review, Georgetown Review, Gulf Coast, Linebreak, Ninth Letter, Pebble Lake Review, Poetry Northwest, Puerto del Sol, Third Coast, Willow Springs*, and *Wigleaf*. Thanks also to the Slash Pine Writers Festival and the Millay Colony for the Arts for their support in the making and discussion of this book and for reprinting excerpts of it in their respective anthology and journal. Thanks to Kristy Bowen, who published "Method of Loci" as a chapbook for dancing girl press.

"Obviator" steals a line from Bobby Jagger. "Love and Forgetting" steals a line from Pablo Neruda. "Spring Elegy" is for Alonzo Kirby.

I owe a debt of gratitude to all the teachers and friends who helped make this book better, especially Peter Streckfus, Wendy Rawlings, and the one-and-only Joel Brouwer. Thanks to Michelle Y. Burke, Elle Collins, Colleen O'Connor, and David Welch for their tireless friendship, insightful reading and regular forgiveness of my neuroses; to my family for their support; and to all the loves of my life for whatever they brought to the table. Lastly, I'm grateful to Black Ocean, Janaka Stucky, and Carrie Olivia Adams for their enthusiasm, eagle eyes and belief in the book.